the last saturday
in america

the last saturday in america

Ray McManus

HUB CITY PRESS
SPARTANBURG, SC

First printing, March 2024
Book design: Kate McMullen
Cover illustration: Joshua Drews

TEXT Adobe Garamond 10.5 / 15
DISPLAY Forma DJR Deck

Library of Congress Cataloging-in-Publication Data

Names: McManus, Ray, 1972- author.
Title: The last Saturday in America / Ray McManus.
Description: Spartanburg, SC : Hub City Press, 2024.
Identifiers: LCCN 2023045187 (print)
LCCN 2023045188 (ebook)
ISBN 9798885740319 (trade paperback) | ISBN 9798885740357 (epub)
Subjects: LCSH: Masculinity--Poetry.
LCGFT: Poetry.
Classification: LCC PS3613.C5853 L37 2024 (print)
LCC PS3613.C5853
(ebook) | DDC 811/.6--dc23/eng/20231005
LC record available at https://lccn.loc.gov/2023045187
LC ebook record available at https://lccn.loc.gov/2023045188

Hub City Press gratefully acknowledges support from the National Endowment for the Arts, the Amazon Literary Partnership, and the South Carolina Arts Commission.

HUB CITY PRESS
186 West Main St.
Spartanburg, SC 29306
1.864.577.9349

for Lindsay, Sean, Morgan, and Lennon

table of contents

introduction

When I was a boy, manhood was a riddle I was hell bent to solve. I knew it smelled like Red Man chewing tobacco and tasted like the beer my father drank. My uncle had rabbit dogs and I figured that was essential, as were pocketknives, overalls, and an exhaust that made the 327 in my father's '67 Camaro sound like that engine could rip apart my house with nothing more than its rumbling.

I spent my entire childhood doing the things that I thought men did. I felled trees, built forts, caught lizards, gutted fish, threw knives, smoked cigarettes, and built fires that got the law called. I shot holes in No Trespassing signs, jumped off railroad trestles, and by most accounts did everything I could to get myself killed. Where I grew up, boys never cried. A dare was a dare. We crossed our hearts and hoped to die. There was no place for backing down.

The search for manhood was very much like climbing a cliff to jump into a lake. Going up isn't bad, but when you get to the edge and your knees are shaking and all you want to do is chicken out, you realize you've gone too far to turn back. There's no way to climb down. All you can do is hurl yourself into the sky and pray to God you hit water.

I look just like my grandfather. That strong chin and nose trickled down through blood, first to my mother then on into me. In the mirror, I see his wiry build, the 6'5" frame that helped him take the Chattanooga Free Press Golden Gloves at 160 pounds in 1940. This is a man who fought in the Second World War, a man who helped build the Blue Ridge Parkway. This is a man I never really knew because he died when I was four. All I remember of him is a single memory, one image that still wakes me from dream: the day he carried snakes.

I couldn't have been more than two or three years old standing beside my mother at the French doors when I saw my grandfather with the snakes. It was the middle of summer and I remember this because of the sound I heard. Summer in the South has a sound and it's the drone of heat bugs, the falling cries of cicadas that start off deafening before slowly fading back into silence.

My grandfather had come from the mountains and was standing in the backyard to help my dad dig out a stump near a tulip poplar. The tree had rotted and fallen and the stump it left was jagged, and my father and grandfather were chopping at the roots with shovels, taking turns trying to rock what was left from the ground. All of a sudden my grandfather knelt and shoved his hands into a break in the clay, first one hand then the other. When he pulled them free there were dozens of baby copperheads writhing in his fists. He stood up and looked to the house, seeming to see me there, me hugging one of my mother's legs, and he smiled while snakes twisted from his fingertips.

The stump must've burned into the night after my father doused it with gasoline and lit both the stump and the snakes afire. I don't remember the flames or the smoke or the smell or anything else about that day or my grandfather, just that single image. But I do remember the charred stump that my father dragged not too deep into the woods being there for my entire childhood like some ashen relic. I do remember the hole in the yard that never leveled out and went years just a red scab of Carolina clay before it finally grew over with grass.

What haunts me still is this fearless confidence that my grandfather had beaming from him, something that even early on I associated with masculinity and manhood, something that despite how hard I've tried, I've never seen in myself. When I dream about this, I wake up sweaty with fear and overcome with feelings of failure. What I saw in my grandfather that day might be the one thing I don't see of him when I look in the mirror, and when I'm entirely honest with myself, I recognize that it's probably the only thing I want to see.

One afternoon years ago, I was back home visiting my parents and was riding with my mother somewhere when she started telling stories about her dad. She said she only ever saw him cry one time in her entire life, and though I expected her to say something along the lines of when he buried his parents, that's not what she said at all.

My mother's eyes glassed over with tears and she said the only time she ever saw him cry was on the day Nat King Cole died. I can remember thinking as soon as she said it how profound that was. For my mother, that was one of the times that defined the man, and when I asked her why, she told me her father always sang, that Nat King Cole had been his favorite. The reality is that it doesn't matter why that singer meant so much to him, or at least it doesn't matter to me. What matters is that it was a moment of tenderness that made him a man in her eyes, and the older I get the more I recognize she's right.

There are times I wonder if I'd witnessed him cry if it would have been the thing I remembered. I think about what I was brought up to believe, what the world taught me about being a man, and though I hate to admit it, I doubt that moment would have been nearly as symbolic had I been there. Knowing what I was taught, I would have probably turned away. That would've been a moment I forced myself to forget, as it would've softened something I'd idealized. If I'd seen him cry, I would've only thought him weak.

Though I never really knew my grandfather, I think it's that fact, the fact that I didn't know him, that allowed me to use the stories I heard and the one image I had to construct some glorified model of masculinity. The man who haunts me, the man who carried snakes, is not my grandfather. He is something created, partly on my own, partly not. Sometimes I wonder if these hardened notions that boys deify are what come to raise violent men, if it's the bottle-it-up, never-cry mentality that leads to why so few of us will ever tell someone how we feel, why none of us feel alright asking for help.

When I was a child, I constructed a cliff from things unsaid, from images quietly observed. I climbed to the ledge and stood where I believed all boys stand, though looking back, no one told me that was where, and maybe that's part of the problem.

The Last Saturday in America is a wrestling of these questions. These are poems about boys listening to men who were once boys who listened to men, the blind leading the blind leading the blind through the dark. Some boys grow up. Some men never do. Ray McManus has chipped away at the pageantry and performance, the stupidity of the lie, the outright futility of it all.

After sitting for a long time trying to make sense of what I wanted to say about this collection I realized that I could not distill it to anything more perfect than two lines Ray'd already written. *The Last Saturday in America* is, "a song that pays homage / to a history of work we should've done better."

Here's hoping one day we do.

David Joy
Author of *Those We Thought We Knew*
Summer 2023

wrasslin'

They come into this world shining,
because in this corner, weighing
in as a last option, boys
are ready to champion the slams of summer.
Like runaway gypsum in the moonlight,
skin slick as birth, part kaolin, part spit,
they'll take what the ground gives them.

The Four Horsemen can't lose.
Dusty Rhodes can't stay cut forever.
Because someone has to be *Stone Cold,*
            so the other can be the *Undertaker.*

Because to beat the count
someone has to shake the hold.

Because like the stars above them,
they're caught in the gaze of the crowd,
indifferent and indignant to the moves
they're pinned in.

Because that's the way
of a shirtless champion
when there's nothing else to lose.

Because like the stars above them,
they're lock-armed against the only backdrop
they've ever known.
Because the turns they'll squirm
to get to the top of the pile.

Because someone has to be the *Ultimate Warrior,*
Vicious has to fight *Superfly,*
Regal has to fight *Animal.*

Because it's American as fuck,
and none of it's real.

I.

angels already know

On the day you are born
God will pull apart husks,
and it will be done outside.
And God will shell peas,
and God will cut melons,
and God will pour salt in the churn
        that God will be watching.

And on the day you are born,
God will put box-fans
on wet windowsills,
a wind-chime in the distance,
and you will be white,
and you will be small,
and the world around
you will be brutal.

But mostly,
you will be small.

where bullies come from

Because you know younger guys
who'd hogtie a boy and not think
anything about leaving him
in a field stripped down
to the Ben-Gay in his jock strap,
go ahead and say it could be worse
because it isn't you.

Because you say we're not born to hate,
that there is no such thing as evil birth,
go ahead and believe that, too,
not because boys will be boys alone
to the dark careful not to shift too hard
or careful not to cut eyes the wrong way
with nothing but faith, just a birth
to a world that is exposed and thirsty,
the look we make when we're helpless,
because you believe that it's necessary
that we are all born to stay born.

Because you say that it's worse to live
with the fact that there are countless ways
to not set foot in a patch of yard
that didn't want you there in the first place,
to do everything you could to not
end up there in the first place, to do something,
anything, that didn't involve the binding
of another human in the first place,
you are saying nothing.
Look past the obvious.

Think about what I am not saying:
maybe one day you'll grow up.
Maybe one day, it will be
the worst thing you've done.

what it takes to stay sober

My dad pokes at the woods and tells me
I can be anything I want to be, I follow him.

He tells me we need the stick for snakes.
He knocks around small brush instead.

For years, we stop where the pines claim
a dry basin, and it's my job to imagine him
when he was younger, how he'd take whatever
water was still there,
                              and his story is always sad,
always marked by trash pile and straw mound,
the cars he never drove,
and eventually he stabs his stick into the ground—
This is why I never drank, he says,
and he leaves me there.

camping with elijah

We called him neighbor,
uncle, the family friend,
I knew him long enough
to not flinch
      when he put his hand on my shoulder
the way he always did
when he told me stories –

     we're all animals he said,
     as we stood behind the tent
     with an empty field watching us.

The story was about chickens and snakes.
How one gives.
How the other takes.

how boys are measured

Because it happens on Black's bridge.

Because someone has to call it,
and since it's night and no one can see,
boys will get pushed to take the next step.

Because there's yelling, the awkward shuffle
in the dark toward the ledge with nothing
to feel in front, just the sound
of the water below swallowing boys
stripped to their skin while the chant:
Too young to use it,
either jump in or lose it
falls to a hush with each jump.

Because there's tension between steps
one and two, front or back, a simple math
where rate is the distance divided by time—
two can't stay in one place forever.

Because on the bridge, boys learn
the arc of man, the depths he must go
for ceremony or shame.

Because on the bridge, boys learn
the stories of those who died
jumping during the drought, and after,
how the constable untangled and stretched
their bodies along the bank—
how he recorded their length
by the steps he took.

hurricane season inland

Because this one: a tree,
a truck, and no seatbelt.
Because we'll have to wait
for toxicology, maybe the weather.
Because we know this road:
  Old Charleston Highway,
  the uphill turn,
  the bloated body in the ditch—
so we call it: drunk kid,
asleep at the wheel,
too young for a bad heart;
too old to listen to anyone who said stay—
  always in a rush they'll say,
  what a waste they'll say,
  we saw this coming.

Because that's the business
of hurricane season—to break
from dead boys in ditches
and prepare for what may never come.

Because that's how we live.
Because that's the prediction
we depend on—a cone of probability
just wide enough
that it might touch us.

Because you'd think
we've gotten used to the tracking
by now—a dozen or so late

summer mornings multiplied
by 17 years, multiplied by 100,
divided by the number of wrecks
between churning furloughs
through sex and heat—
same face,
same words,
every year,
the same year.

Because the truth is,
we won't see a drop from this system—
we won't even feel
the wind coming or going.

Because even when disappointed,
a weatherman's face can make it easy
to forget that some kids die alone
like that, face-down and whispering
against rising water.

we know the field

Because we know the path along the firebreak
that cuts through pines where it's safe to slip past
transfer-trucks to get behind the dumpster unnoticed.

Because we know that's where we'll find a girl
too pretty for us, too pretty to be slinging plates
for the late shift at the 44 Truck Stop.

Because we know an angel when we see one.

Because we know she'll teach us how to pray
before taking the bottle from her throat to wash our feet.

Because we know on Saturday nights, when flesh tightens
around the rib and aches for touch, men will come
with sacks of silver to drop from the nearby auto auction.

Because we know despite the bill she'll tell us to be patient,
and we will, and we'll take turns watching the world
around us scream and fall apart as it dies
to the hum of old songs spilling from tired engines.

when the men are talking

Past the lawn chair, the fire pit,
where the nearest bridge is;

and the voices that ask

past the lighter

tossed to the ground;

past the wives

inside at the kitchen table,
their glasses near full
as they sip,
each a deliberate murmur;

past the silence among them;
past the night itself
or the day before

when most of the men watched
the Savings & Loan
from across the street
and admitted, one by one,
how much money
it would take to rob it;

past the admission by some
that it wouldn't take much;

past the week before that,
past months;
past years;
past the time

the story of one's limp;

some of these men gathered
behind the school
where they found the body
of a little boy just days before
and someone thought
it was good idea to pray
for guidance moving forward,
and they did;

past two decades before that,

past the burn barrel

past his hand that shakes;
past the glow against his jaw;
past the shadow on the scar
   below it;

a different yard,
a different time,
when you learned the price
of speaking out
when you're 11
and there's hog killing;
and the oldest man standing—
the WWII vet
who reminds everyone
that he has seen colder;

look,
and then look past it.

on the road to damascus

Because some things don't show up on maps:
the midlands, farms dried out, all the years
we've plowed under going back and forth
letting the dust settle where it falls,
and from that dust, white boys are born
to get lucky or to fill their parents' ashtrays,
whichever comes first.

Because there's no maps for hand-me-downs,
there's no key for ghosts, just a hand to push
the sand to the side and a foot to drag through it.

Because it doesn't take much to turn
a game trail into a foot-path into a logging tract,
then field, then pen—a house here, a shed there,
then the trailers, and then us—the unpaved and unwashed,
and if we're lucky, we'll be scraped down
to broken bottle, rusted buckle, the bleached bones
of wild dogs, something old, something confederate.

Because sometimes we'll get to a spot where we can
pass jars and sacks between us and the chicken houses.

Because sometimes we hear the rattle of a car bumper
banging ruts before we ever see the headlights,
and sometimes we don't.

Because sometimes we're born to spend the better part
of our lives staring at unpainted walls in prison.

Because sometimes we'll drop
concrete blocks off bridges onto highways.

Because sometimes we'll push
letter-openers into the throats of girlfriends who lived
for a weekend at best tweaked and scattered
on the couch of someone else's Saturday night.

Because sometimes we'll forget how many
blind curves eat dirt roads, and we'll lose count
as to how many trucks hug pine trees
or the number of teeth the coroner extracts.

Because it's easy here to see the best way to go nowhere
is through the dark with our hands behind our backs.

Because it's easy here to wonder
what the other side of dust feels like.

Because it's easy here to think
that the best way to make do is don't.

when you can't tell the vine
from the branches

Because you bought the only plot you could afford—
the half-acre of scrub oak, just off the dirt road—
you hate it.

Because you hate the smell of paint,
want the Sunday morning
to stand-alone.
        Not the chain.
        Not the all-night drive-through.

Because you want the muscle
of a jacked-up God
being praised in a Walmart Revival
that's good enough for American lawns.

Because you carry.

Because you conceal.

        Look down.
        Always look down.

fuck it

for Worth

Because you don't care about the job as long as it pays.

Because everyone has to jump in a hole, and everyone has to reach
for a neck to find a plug to drain a pan to scrape out a trap.

The boss's son doesn't have to jump
in anything because he drives a clean truck.

Because you think one day you will too.

Because you're face down in a crawl-space digging through
another man's shit with gravel pushed against your belly.

Because one day, you'll have time to tamp out
your blessings but they won't be near enough.

Because nothing just falls towards the mouth
the way light cuts the evening as it creeps up the driveway.

Because tiny fingers push down window blinds, and eyes squint
for your shadow, eyes that don't know the word *quit*.

the dale earnhardt school of human experience

Because you win some
when it comes to this race,
but let's be upfront about it—
you can't commit
to making the turns
if you don't claim the inside.

Because you lose some
to the ones who think
it's best to slow down,
that cars should stay
parked in driveways,
that backyards are where
kids should scream as they run.

Because you wreck some
days and burn down others,
drive into town
like a mother-fucker anyway,
position the kids
to look out the car window,
and dare them to witness everything.

calculus for a disappearing south

There are more than enough dirt roads
    in the South to bury a body deeper than the one before.

        How much distance is needed
        for a car traveling 47 miles an hour to cave in
        a shoulder when a road scraper is present?

Start with nothing.
    Start with entire albums.

    Start in the back
    through the smoke
    and hiss of 6x9 speakers,
    and take every rut,
    every wash-boarded ripple,
    and call it Friday night.

Multiply the distance by body weight.

The next night, take the holes,
and repeat the trek until out of gas or out of beer.

    Mark it as graduation.
        Solve X by Y,
        where X is the road and Y is the sandpit.

    Divide by the number
    of friends who died there.

    Carry the one.

Solve for square root.
  Circle common denominator.
  Bury what you can.

The names become the numbers,
  the dust subtracting
    what you're told.

These are variables that like to stay hidden,
because there's nothing to hold,
just bits that float through the canopy
of scrub-oak and loblolly
like ash that scatters in the wind.

    Sometimes, it lands in your mouth.
    Sometimes, you swallow.

II.

how to forget a nation

My first mistake was the row of rocks
used to mark the border
My second mistake was showing you.

Rocks, I explained, leave a mark.
That, too, was a mistake.

Tonight, I'll move them back.
In all honesty, I have no idea where they go.
I say this facing the dark
because it's easier to lie that way.

What do I know about rocks or borders?
I don't know where they come from,
why they're just sitting here waiting
for someone like me to pick one up
and rub the flat side, the messy side.

I don't even know which side is which.
Like most men, I never thought to ask.

origin of species

My neighbor was born 400,000 years ago
and crawled in the grass because food
was dangerous. He learned math and tables
because the cat takes the bird, the bird takes
the fish. Because there is safety in numbers.
Because he will always be hungry.

My neighbor evolved into a hand hidden
in a bathrobe, an arm that could swing
when raised, but at night he strips
in the open and lets what falls lie.

How easy it would be to call him savage
in his ape-like sway, the way he swings a stick
around the yard, the rocks in his pocket.

How easy it would be to think
that a hand should mean something
if neighbors are going to eat each other.

But apes don't look for rocks to keep.
Apes don't need math. They don't carry
a stick hoping for a chance to use it.

the give and take

The line starts every exhibit, one display then the next,
always an origin, always a narrative in stop motion,
how one simple movement stretches toward epoch,
how time gives in to the excuses we make,
how men raise their arms to push back the sky,
how the sky lets them trophy a familiar privilege.

Museums work like that, build monuments
out of what's given and what's taken away.

We've seen the mammoth, the contents of its stomach.
We've seen the blankets behind the glass, and know
who shivers in the dark and who doesn't.

Every exhibit, one display and then the next,
lines for a narrative, a song that pays homage
to a history of work we should've done better.

in the museum of men and their machines

Says here that manual transmissions are metaphors
for a man who is too tight and demanding, can't get right.

Says here a man's fluid should be checked often
to soften the shift from muted to rooted then ground.

Says here a man cannot eat fire so he curses through it
and runs hot, jammed, slammed, and goddamned. In gear.

Says here the brain begets God—not the other way around—
and the body begets bible, but only one bleeds in the bed

at night. Says here a man tightens timing and blames break-
downs in viscosity as one in the same, has no skin in the game

but insists on driving anyway. Says here a man snaps
where he can't bend, tends to over-extend, too willing

to give in to exhaust. Says here men ignore machine wear
and tear and fuck up everything. Says here it's normal.

how to stay bent

After we made love
against a wall behind
the Early Tool and Die exhibit,
my wife told me how
nails were harder to make
because men came easy.

I joked that we must've fallen
in love for that very reason,
but she didn't laugh,
not when there are millions
of men just lying around
with no special purpose,
a dime for a dozen
in the swells of presentation.

If not for her face,
I wouldn't know the history
of men who burned their house down.
I wouldn't know the widows
who waited until the embers cooled
to collect the nails needed for rebuilding.

She knows I only have one history,
one where men prefer tying
the legs of other men to trees
and driving nails through their wrists.

She said it wasn't necessarily
the dumbest way
to hold a man together.

Then she laughed.

black and white cowboys

After cartoons, it's black and white: someone has to die and someone else has to stand there and watch it, but it's never enough to stop the commercials. What's the point of complicating cruelty when there's money to be made?

The boys judge what's good or bad by the only colors they're given: there's a white man in a white hat. He beats the dust off his thighs, reaches down with his index finger toward the trigger, and takes the ground from under the other man's feet.

Color makes no difference to the dead, but the boys see good guys and bad guys marked by contrast and brightness. They confuse it with what's left standing and what's left to bleed, as scripted, as directed, as advertised.

Soon they will yell and squeal and cheer, ready to re-enact what they saw, ready to turn on each other by the closing credits. And we'll be relieved if they just do it outside where we can see them.

natural selection

Cats patrol my neighborhood.
They roam slack-back and don't give a shit.
Always one or two, rarely more than,
following each other at a purposeful distance.
They cross the street heads up. Stodgy and smug.
Cool and beautiful. And I fucking hate them.

My neighbor, from across the street sees me,
walks over looking at the tabby squeezing
into the drainage culvert. "He's the sassy one,"
she says, "the book says so." She tells me
she was an art teacher at an all-girls college
in the northeast. She tells me how she's retired,
taking care of her 93-year-old father,
how she reads books about cats on her porch.

She asks me some questions: what do I do to live,
how many kids eat here, can I believe the weather
we're having. But before I can answer, she moves on
to something else, tells me how she takes
photographs of trash on the side of the road
(doesn't say whether she picks it up after),
how her husband can barely walk these days,
and she complains about the irregularity of mail.
I quit trying to speak and leave her running
commentary to the sunset. Two more cats slip
into the culvert. "I don't like the dark one,"
she says, "it's always teasing the dogs at night."

man's greatest hits

Side A:
                    It's enough
to make our fathers sad
for the day when a nation
can no longer perform
the way it used to.
                    Not one animal
eating another,
                    but each animal
                        eating each other.
Not one nation under,
but over,
as in over,
as in done,
                    where we no longer
have to hide our souls
in the woods behind a church to die,
                    how we live
defined
                    by
what we chew on
and what we swallow.

Side B:
                    The songs
you'd expect to hear.
                    The rest:
                    shitty covers.

boomer

My neighbor is all tongue and twisted lip,
all plastic hip and napalm,
all belt and broken motor,
a gift, some might say, from a heartless god.

And at the hottest part of the day
when most of us have taken
to quieter comforts, he stands
in his yard pistol tight
and ready to take out snakes.

My neighbor was born a Cadillac,
not a Caprice Classic, not a Cutlass Supreme,
an ornament unhooded, all back surgery
and wrecking ball, all bumper bent around a frame.

His face searches for the shadow from his visor.
He races backwards as if it's better than standing still.
His Saturday evenings are wrecked
by kids not yet bound by imaginary lines.
And my neighbor will blame me
for poor slope and lack of backfill,
how rocks are not brick,
how the voices of my children crash
through his window.

But my neighbor doesn't talk like a parent,
doesn't work the angles
the way we should when we're scared.

My neighbor is all Rambo and Vronsky,
all blood in the throat,
all hard bark before it falls to the ground.

Snakes, like kids mostly, are harmless,
like neighbors when left alone.

And some say snakes are just
looking for a nest that's not like home,
a place to rest if swollen after a meal.
Sometimes they get stuck there.

Everything is capable of being.
Everything is capable of being unwanted.
My neighbor has been here longer than anyone,
longer than a neighborhood or a heartless god,
longer than a bullet.

My neighbor is the wind that dies on a face.

My neighbor says hello when he sees a snake
stretched next to the tree line, and kills it anyway.

My neighbor is all fist for the right-handed,
all tumor and revolt, all pit and strike.

He'll be here longer than anyone.
Just ask the snake.

whatever the opposite of extinction is

Like most men,
I pretend to know
what I am talking about
when I mark my territory,
fire a shot through the stern,
declare war as a matter of diplomacy.

Like most men,
I confuse occupation
and domestic agenda,
swell against polyester
for nylon, wage war
on portion control,
but when my wife puts her fork down
and asks me what's wrong
with my mouth,
I bit off more than I can chew
and swallow my food whole.

I know the intention of pitch,
the risk of inflection, the point
between posture and pander,
but my mouth, foul from roof to corner,
has been the staging point
for nearly every invasion.

It's all the talk
of caves and castles,
the meat in my hand,
and battlefield commissions that swell

my tongue, that leave me to insist
on talking in the first place.

And like most men,
I've been quick
to shoot the messenger.

Like most men,
I've evolved
just enough.

empty church

We were marked and didn't even know it.
We lived by avoiding eye contact, nights like this one,
when the autumn air falls on the skin just long enough

for a man to feel needed, to chop and drag and forget
the short lengths of days yet to pass. We passed
by not knowing the cost, a price still not paid in full,

like earlier today, when our youngest daughter found lizards
sunning through the slats of the pergola. She named them,
made them homes. She doesn't watch the news, or know

the diction we've spilt on the counter, the corners
we cut in the clean-up, the manufactured grace
it takes to teeter between life and death because

of a simple choice we make to hold back breath or blow.
What I would give to unknow, to unthink, to not speak
of a tomorrow or a next week; I just know we can't

have reptiles running around in the house. Tonight,
against the first frost of the year, the fire we built will go
out simply because we didn't tend to it. It has nothing

to do with a war on impending darkness. We'll sleep in
our bed, because our daughter is safe between us and the cold.
And by morning, maybe all the lizards will be dead.

any morning but saturday

The boys wake up at 6, ready to fight their sister while I bark at the sun. She's already at the table claiming what shouldn't be hers by birth because she's the youngest, because that's just the way it is. Call it sibling rivalry. Like breakfast was cold, like the bus stop, despite their hair in a tangled nest of every morning we've ever had, like salmon and grits and liver pudding and toast, like mornings with thick oatmeal or cream of wheat – whatever was done was done on time, and stuck there. Call it legacy. Like mornings they race to not brush their teeth after I use the bathroom. Like mornings I stop them in the hallway to give them the last three dollars I have. Like mornings they stare at their plates while I stand in the den and strip down to my skin and tell them about cancer.

I am hardly dead,
just naked, cold, and watching
them fight for my clothes.

manifest destiny

For the pump of it,
the drop, the brake, the tongue,
the asshole, the nipple pointed
against the sunlight under the visor—
  I'll be the first to admit it,
  I'll do anything
  for a new sun to shimmer
  before it explodes into a million suns.
For all that's left of you and me to cool the engine.
For the ride on the two-lane past the swamp,
  past the blockhouses and garages where boys break
  radios to fan belt overtures before they die.
For the fact that I know I won't miss them
       and never did.

For the damp of it.
For the turns we'll take where imaginations race shadows,
and I'll think what I could do if I could be you if you just let me
  and you let me.
For the grind it takes to be an engine.
For the timing it takes to turn everything over,
  to stay tuned,
  to stay hard,
  to stay tuned again—
    this isn't magic.
This isn't a mystery either—
  compression,
  fire,
  the death that comes from the exhaust of it,
  from the boredom of it.

In town, people look the same, wear the same,
speak in same to same. It's all the same:
no machines to wrestle, no boys waiting
to die in open bays. Just windows stuffed
with paper, vinyl covering the brick.

In town, people keep their hands to themselves,
train their eyes to see both ways before crossing—
bodies shaped to live cautious and deliberate—
but they never look.
     This can't be *my* country.

For the love of it, the pledge of it,
the word for it,
     this has to be *our* country.

For the destination we'll reach in union.
For ratification.
For surges between the scar and the shoulder.
For a nation we should've forgotten in the first place.
For the fastest route from savagery to decadence.
For my palm and your palm at the edge of the swamp.
For what we'll call *here*.
For what we'll call *now*.
   Here, where we can't trick out the word.
   Now, where there is no word.
Just you and me by our divine right,
surveying the space between us,
   taking it,
     and calling it ours.

how the west is won

for Matthew Olzmann

Because you show no mercy for a small killing, just drop chicken on our plates and watch us eat. Because when the kids sleep, you crouch in the darkest corner of their bedroom, where the smells of their feet can't distract you from watching the movement of their bellies.

Because you take your stand at the kitchen window, when I want to piss in the sink.

Because you see a faint punch of light against a cold night, and joke that you know the kind of men who'd sit around a fire and let you pull the graveyard taste from their mouths. (That is a joke, right?)

Because when I said we should move to Akron, you didn't budge. And when I said we should move to Dallas, you didn't budge. And when I said we should move to Sligo, you didn't budge. Because you don't budge for my bullshit—like the time you placed your hand on my chest to stop me from beating a man to death who almost ran over our entire family in the Publix parking lot.

Because later, you whispered in my ear that it turns you on when I bag our groceries myself.

Because you know I like it when you lie—like when the kids leave for school, and we get to break our savage hearts against each other, and 15 minutes later you rework the notches on your belt and adjust your holster for a showdown in a boardroom at high noon.

Because you tell me you appreciate me taking the time.

Because I know you're not the type to wait for a man to slow-walk his paces.

Because you'll shoot first, from the hip if necessary, and when it's November, it's stays November, and you will put food on the table any way you can kill it.

Because there was that time, two summers ago, when you could have died, or the 8 years before that, when doctors couldn't stop the bleeding and you should have died, and your only real worry was that no one was eating.

Because you put the meat in our stomachs, not God, and before we eat anything, when we hold our hands for grace, you rub your thumb over the top of my busted knuckle.

III.

one way to tame a dog

The joke started
when I was nine, maybe ten,
when dad came back
from the woods with blood
on his boots. The dog's tumors,
the worms—logical reasons
to justify seven gunshots.

I don't know how that was a joke,
or what compels me to talk
about my dad, or why I feel
the need to tell my wife how
he never told me the joke about bulls
on a hill looking down on cows,
or why I just like the way she tells it.

My instinct tells me this is how we play,
how one pulls against the other,
that I talk too much and that's why
my skin is cold under the ceiling fan.

Like a puppy that doesn't know
when to shut up, so I'll burrow
into my wife's skin when she calls
for me and I'll let her eat away
at what's left every single time.

My dad never told me that joke either.

survey

A river has to start somewhere.

Heavy with a body pulling under
and the air between spilling where it wants,
like breath that dies on the skin,
the conversations of old friends buried
in the fog at dawn. What starts
as a simple act of nature becomes
the current that carries our fathers,
and their fathers before that, falls,
and fails in the end the way ghosts do.

My wife asks how deep is it.
This is how we are born, I tell her.

We could move anywhere if it weren't
for the kids, so we move when we can,
where we can. The best we can.
This is how we are born here.
Blood song and mountain, the pool,
the push, the flatland, slick bush.

So I say not deep enough, not even
a hill to climb. And she's ok with that.

Soon the love of majesty ends
and a river, for all its simple words,
is a midland wish that we will die
before we ever reach the ocean.
The kids sleep in their own rooms.

My wife stays on top; I stay somewhere
on the bottom. Water falls from her
body onto mine. I want to drown in it.

night fishing

My wife and I have been at it
for hours and still no bite.
I want to tell her
that the bait slipped,
that I really hate fishing
where I can't see.
But she wants me to tell her
my theory again,
the one about men just being
fish lured by big water—
that they know a hook
when they see one.

It's more of a story really.
Something all men share
at some point in the drink.
Men swim slower
when there's no sun
to charm them blind,
no machines to churn
the lots behind them,
no iron pipes to crush
them into the concrete
before a daughter's first birthday.

But the truth is, it's bullshit.
Men tend to toss
a lazy cast because it's easy
to forget that a hook is brutal
for a reason. And fish, as dumb

as they are in their approach,
rarely make that mistake twice.

Tomorrow night, we'll try again.

smoke signals

We could use a translator
on most days.
Sundays to be exact
when my wife floats
over the earth
and I sink into a chair.

How do you say *soft skin?*
What's the word for *hair* or *hide?*

She touches the side
of my face and sets a plate
on my lap. In the middle,
a skin sack stuffed
with organs pulled tight
and tied at the top.

I accept her offering,
even if I'm not quite sure
what to do with it.
Even if my mouth could hold
more than I know,
it is always open.

How do you point
to the back of the throat
and say *kill it?*

How do you say *right here?*

there is a risk of swelling, bruising, and tenderness

The pamphlets say *safe*, say *easy*,
say most men, say *normal, typical,*
and *often* and with ease, the way
print fingers the crease but stays
out of the fold. Fonts with no stake.
Baseless men in toothy pictures
comfortable with their vasectomies.
Women smiling. They say *non-invasive*;
they say *minimal*. Blonde captions.

Sedation, prescriptions, and weekend
recovery. In that order. The doctor
will like the word easy and say it
as if he knows I like it. No sentence.
Just a three-day weekend and ice.
And this is his waiting room. No place
for the quiet. And the television.
The commercials we stare at.
The home improvement we seek.

Let's do this: let's ignore the power
of doing. I can be the wind that pushes
back the curtain and falls to the side
of the bed. I can say *the end*, and you
can say *thank you*. And when the curtain
falls into place, only a part of me goes
and doesn't come back. A small part.

pioneer diorama

I have no idea what the Friday girls are selling
in the trailer on the hill. Looks like stuff
they bought then made. Bags maybe.

My wife is a native here. She says
she can scrape out a stomach
and make me a bag if I want one.
She said the same thing yesterday.

She says this in Choctaw
with her face against the glass.
The girls on the hill don't notice.
They have no idea how close they are
to dying. How they will.

Tonight, our children will cough in their beds
and dream of an exhibit
we once called *The American Weekend.*

Tomorrow will just be
another day for me to hunt the backyard
and kill everything I see.

And the day after,
I'll wake to find bones
arranged by shape and color,
skins draped over the rail to dry.

And I'll plow.
And I'll plant.

And I'll stand
in that field
with my mouth shut.

And I'll be cured.

post op

We're riding lighter
on the way back.

You're driving
and telling me
the dream you had
the night before –
I ask if I can smoke
and then you die.
It's a horrible dream.

I should ask
if that's what weighs
on you the most,
but I do that thing
where I try to say that
what you feel I feel,
and then somehow
it comes back to me.

We ride the rest
of the way home
holding hands
in silence toward
a dark horizon.

Your dreams in your lap,
the numbness in mine.

homo habitus

Because I'd like to say,
        I haven't changed.
        But evolution doesn't work that way.

Because I'm here now,
      in this cut-out landscape
      of row-houses and cul-de-sacs
          where there once was a field
          where there once was a forest,
          where boys and girls run in separate packs,
          where it's everyone for themselves,
               and we hide from our neighbors
               and keep their tools
               because it's too damn hot
               to go outside anymore.

Because I pay for cable. All of it.
The bundles, the half-off deals,
the premium channels, the turbo, the super-
strength, the warp-speed, and I stare out
the window with my thumb on the remote
because there is nothing on the television.

And I'm dying here.
        Every day.

Because I'd like to say,
        with the same confidence,
        that I'm coming back,
        that this is just another trip

too long or too many,
where I take a right
when I should take a left,
or don't, and sit somewhere,
sit here, and ache with a wedge
in my lap to negotiate
simple things:

the lung, the bladder,
and how I can change what I see
in a matter of seconds,
and how I can't.

Because the truth is I can wait here forever;
I don't even have to come back
because I never left in the first place.

Because this is worship.
This is worship for Colonel Steve Austin.
For McGarret and Rockford.
For Charles Ingalls and Ponch.
For Henry Blake and Magnum.
For the worship and praise for everyman.

Every channel.
Every day.

Because on bended knee,
there will be the belief in the buy-in,
there will be the belief in the shift,
how it can only get better.

All the ethos. All the pageantry.

    All the prophets and the profits
that we doubt in the rise,
and we sift in the fall,
because how else would we know
when we are so wild with our sorrow?

Because I'd like to say,
                with the same faith,
                        a complete man exists.
He is the dark and the light.
He is the force that burns out
      apartments and spits at the sky
      while the rest of us hide
            because we can't speak,
            can't speak of it,
            don't want to.

Praise you Oxiclean.
Praise you Just For Men.
Praise you Clearasil.
Praise you Kitchen Crashers.
Praise you Polident.
Praise you Behr paints exclusively at Home Depot.
Praise you McRib.
Praise you Bowflex and the Total Gym.
Praise you Botox and AndroGel.

Because now I know I'll never wear the cape.
Because now I know I'll never carry gods on my shoulders.

And I'll let the word
            of commercial Jesus
            fall from my lips.
And I'll wear his stains
            like badges, like lyrics
            scrawled on my shirt.

Because I can.
Because I can always be here,
            new and improved.

nobody's bargain

I watch her and she watches me
moving from office to den,
to back yard, and then den
to office to back yard again,
the side grin between sliding
glass doors, then office to kitchen
to den to bathroom to office to bed,
and then the morning comes. Fast.
Another day moves faster
than the one before, until it feels
like it's not moving at all.

And there's mornings
where we yell because another day
moves louder than the one before
until it forces us to scream our words
if we have anything to say.

And I hear her. And she hears me
moving from pantry to fridge
to stove to porch to stove again,
running into furniture
and cursing the ash on the carpet.

And I hear her ask what's wrong.
And she hears me say nothing.
Because my throat hurts,
and I don't know if I can smell
what's cooking or burning
and nothing can distract me

from the fact I could be responsible
for killing everyone in this house.
Or my neighbor's house.
Or my parents. Or her parents.
Or the cashier at Lowe's foods,
where I bought a beer
and walked around the store
sometime in early Spring
thinking about how much
I liked seeing some of the people
in Jasper County Georgia.
How easy it was then
to not know anything and just feel,
to think distance required agency,
to see food on the shelves.

And it's at that moment,
when I start to question
what I cannot taste before
I even put it in my mouth,
that I feel her hand on my back.

And it's at that moment
she feels me let go and breathe
as I look through the door of the stove.
Smells good she says.

And I'll be damned, she's right.

the last saturday in america

If my neighbor slams his shovel to the ground
and stomps across the yard toward the gas can,
I should let him. We're not friends,
but I offer him water, which he takes,
and we talk about roots, good dirt, how
that limb just fell one day, the black spot
that ate its way down the middle of the trunk.
I can't ever remember his name.

Across the street, the neighborhood stray sniffs
the fence line. The new people moved here
two weeks ago. They keep their dog chained
to the trampoline. My neighbor is quick
to recognize a bitch in heat, says someone needs
to get that dog fixed or shoot it, and then he's back
to the fire he started. The stray – clearly male,
matted and thin and desperate for the wreck –
claws at the dirt and bites at the gate. It doesn't take
long for him realize that it's easier to jump
over the fence than it is to crawl under it.
My neighbor never looks up.

I won't tell him that he can't burn a stump out
that way. I won't tell him that it's easier to cover
and leave it to rot, that he'd be better off blowing
the whole thing up and just fill in the hole later.
I won't tell him his wife is at the window, watching.

diehards

I'm dying.
My wife is dying.
Our kids are dying.
Their pets are dying.

The neighbors are dying.
The tree out back is dying,
and the field behind it
is dying again.

The road is not dying,
but everything on it is:
every bone cycle,
every skin machine,
and that's where
we're leaving it.

My wife pats the backseat,
wakes the kids and says look.
Their eyes are wide open
in the rearview mirror.

acknowledgments

A deep appreciation to the editors of these journals, sites, and anthologies who published these poems:

Binder: "Empty Church"
Cold Mountain Review: "Whatever the Opposite of Extinction Is"
Dead Mule School of Southern Literature: "Origin of Species"
Fall Line: "Where Bullies Come From," "When You Can't Tell the Vines from the Branches"
Good Men Project: "How Boys are Measured" and "Survey"
Healing Muse: "There is a Risk of Swelling, Bruising, and Tenderness," "Post Op"
James Dickey Review: "Calculus for a Disappearing South," "How to Stay Bent," and "One Way to Tame a Dog"
Open-Eyed and Full-Throated: "Manifest Destiny," "Boomer" (as Caveman Bias), "Diehards," and "How to Forget a Nation"
POETRY: "Diehards"
Salvation South: "Angels Already Know," "We Know the Field," "The Dale Earnhardt School of Human Experience," "The Last Saturday in America"
San Pedro River Review: "Hurricane Season Inland," "How the West Is Won"
storySouth: "Night Fishing"
Talking River Literary Journal: "Smoke Signals," "When the Men are Talking"
The South Carolina Review: "In the Museum of Men and Their Machines," "Homo Habitus"
Twelve Mile Review: "On the Road to Damascus," "Wrasslin'"
Ukweli: "Black and White Cowboys"
What Things Cost: "Fuck It"
Yemassee: "What It Will Take to Stay Sober"

So much of this book would not be possible if not for the people in my life; some have no idea how much they meant to me while I was writing it.

I love you all, David Joy, Nickole Brown, Beth Ann Fennelly, BJ Barham, Ed Madden, Kwame Dawes, Jillian Weise, Sean Thomas Dougherty, George Singleton, Nathalie Anderson, John Lane, Ashley M Jones, Hobart Trotter, Tom DeLoach, Jessica Jacobs, Dawn Hyde, Dan Turner, Joelle Ryan Cook and Drew Baron and all the amazing folks at the Columbia Museum of Art, Rick Fitts, my wonderful colleagues at University of South Carolina Sumter, of course the incomparable folks at Hub City Press.

I'd be dead if weren't for my children Sean, Morgan, and Lennon, and most definitely my wife, Lindsay Green McManus, who is my first reader and my love always.

And lastly, the neighbors: you know who you are, and you are part of us.

PUBLISHING
New & Extraordinary
VOICES FROM THE
AMERICAN SOUTH

HUB CITY PRESS is a non-profit independent press in Spartanburg, SC that publishes well-crafted, high-quality works by new and established authors, with an emphasis on the Southern experience. We are committed to high-caliber novels, short stories, poetry, plays, memoir, and works emphasizing regional culture and history. We are particularly interested in books with a strong sense of place.

Hub City Press is an imprint of the non-profit Hub City Writers Project, founded in 1995 to foster a sense of community through the literary arts. Our metaphor of organization purposely looks backward to the nineteenth century when Spartanburg was known as the "hub city," a place where railroads converged and departed.

RECENT HUB CITY PRESS POETRY

El Rey of Gold Teeth • Reyes Ramirez

In the Hands of the River • Lucien Darjeun Meadows

Thresh & Hold • Marlanda Dekine

Reparations Now! • Ashley M. Jones

Sparrow Envy • J. Drew Lanham

Adobe Garamond Pro
10.5 / 14